Collins
INTERNATIONAL PRIMARY

Wellbeing
Student's Book 1

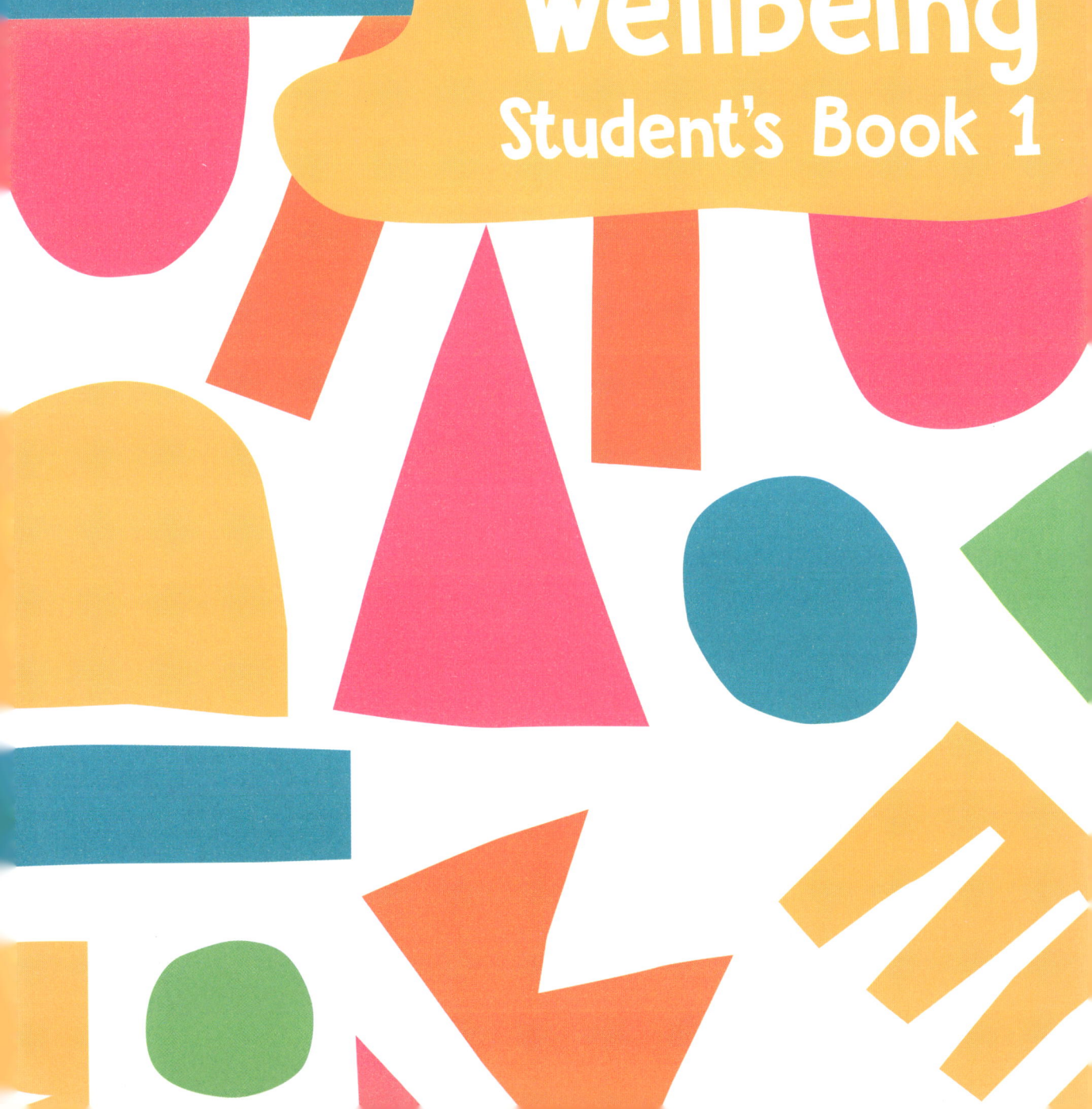

William Collins' dream of knowledge for all began with the publication of his first book in 1819.

A self-educated mill worker, he not only enriched millions of lives, but also founded a flourishing publishing house. Today, staying true to this spirit, Collins books are packed with inspiration, innovation and practical expertise.

They place you at the centre of a world of possibility and give you exactly what you need to explore it.

Collins. Freedom to teach.

Published by Collins

An imprint of HarperCollins*Publishers*
The News Building, 1 London Bridge Street, London,
SE1 9GF, UK

HarperCollins*Publishers*
Macken House, 39/40 Mayor Street Upper, Dublin 1 D01 C9W8

Browse the complete Collins catalogue at
collins.co.uk

© HarperCollins*Publishers* Limited 2024

10 9 8 7 6 5 4 3 2 1

ISBN 978-0-00-864518-2

British Library Cataloguing-in-Publication Data
A catalogue record for this publication is available from the British Library.

Cambridge International copyright material in this publication is reproduced under licence and remains the intellectual property of Cambridge University Press & Assessment.

Third-party websites and resources referred to in this publication have not been endorsed by Cambridge International Education.

Endorsement indicates that a resource has passed Cambridge International Education's rigorous quality-assurance process and is suitable to support the delivery of a Cambridge curriculum framework. However, endorsed resources are not the only suitable materials available to support teaching and learning, and are not essential to achieve the qualification. Resource lists found on the Cambridge website will include this resource and other endorsed resources.

Any example answers to questions taken from past question papers, practice questions, accompanying marks and mark schemes included in this resource have been written by the authors and are for guidance only. They do not replicate examination papers. In examinations the way marks are awarded may be different.

Any references to assessment and/or assessment preparation are the publisher's interpretation of the curriculum framework requirements. Examiners will not use endorsed resources as a source of material for any assessment set by Cambridge International Education.

While the publishers have made every attempt to ensure that advice on the qualification and its assessment is accurate, the official curriculum framework, specimen assessment materials and any associated assessment guidance materials produced by the awarding body are the only authoritative source of information and should always be referred to for definitive guidance.

Our approach is to provide teachers with access to a wide range of high-quality resources that suit different styles and types of teaching and learning.

For more information about the endorsement process, please visit www.cambridgeinternational.org/endorsed-resources

Series editor: Kate Daniels
Author: Victoria Pugh
Publisher: Elaine Higgleton
Product manager: Cathy Martin
Product developer: Roisin Leahy
Development and copy editor: Jo Kemp
Proofreader: Claire Throp
Illustrations: Jouve India Ltd.
Cover designers: Amparo Barrera, Kneath Associates and Gordon MacGilp
Typesetter: Sam Vail, Ken Vail Graphic Design
Production controller: Sarah Hovell
Printed and bound by Martins

MIX
Paper | Supporting
responsible forestry
FSC
www.fsc.org
FSC™ C007454

This book is produced from independently certified FSC™ paper to ensure responsible forest management.

For more information visit: www.harpercollins.co.uk/green

We are grateful to the following teachers for providing feedback on the resources as they were developed:
Ms Hema Gehani and Ms Seema Desai at Colours Innovation Academy, Ms Manjari Tennakoon and Ms Surani Maithripala at Gateway Colleges, and Preeti Roychoudhury, Farishta Dastur Mukerji, Spriha Patronobis and Sukonna Halder at Calcutta International School and Vicky Walsh, at Vicky Walsh Education.

Contents

Hello and welcome to your Wellbeing Stage 1 Student's Book.

Let's take a quick look at what is inside.

Feelings

Starting school can be exciting! But you might feel lots of other different things too, like feeling shy or scared or worried. Because you are in a classroom with lots of other children it is important to understand their feelings too. This book will help you understand more about both your feelings and those of other people.

Understanding yourself

The activities in your book will help you find out what makes you happy or sad and what helps you if you are feeling angry or upset. There is a lot you can do to help yourself feel better.

Being healthy

Being healthy is very important, so we will look at exercise, eating well and teeth brushing in this section!

Family and friends

Getting on well with other people at home and in the classroom is important too because it helps us be happy. So we are going to have a look at how to do this too.

Keeping safe

Learning to look after yourself in school and when you are outside will keep you safe. And working through these workbooks will help!

Growing up

You are growing up and starting school is a big step towards growing up. Let's look at what growing up means.

Being special

Finally, we are going to take a look at what makes you special. Because you are special!

I hope you enjoy your wellbeing Student's Book.

May your year be as wonderful as you are!

Becky Goddard-Hill

Unit 1.1 How do I feel?

What do you know?

● What can you see in the picture?

● Can you tick the emojis that show feelings you have felt at some time?

In this unit, you will:

● Create emotion stones.

● Think of ways to help a friend when they are experiencing big emotions.

● Explore what empathy means.

Lesson 1 My feelings

Activity 1.1a My feelings

What makes you feel happy, sad and excited? Write your answers below and say why these things make you feel this way.

I feel happy when _____

_____

_____

because _____

_____

_____

_____

I feel sad when _____

_____

_____

because _____

_____

_____

_____

I feel excited when _____

_____

_____

because _____

_____

_____

Lesson 1 My feelings

Activity 1.1b When I feel angry

Draw or write things you could do to calm yourself down when you feel angry.

Lesson 1 My feelings

Activity 1.1c Emotion stones

Decorate each pebble with a different emotion. Think about the shapes, colours and details you might use.

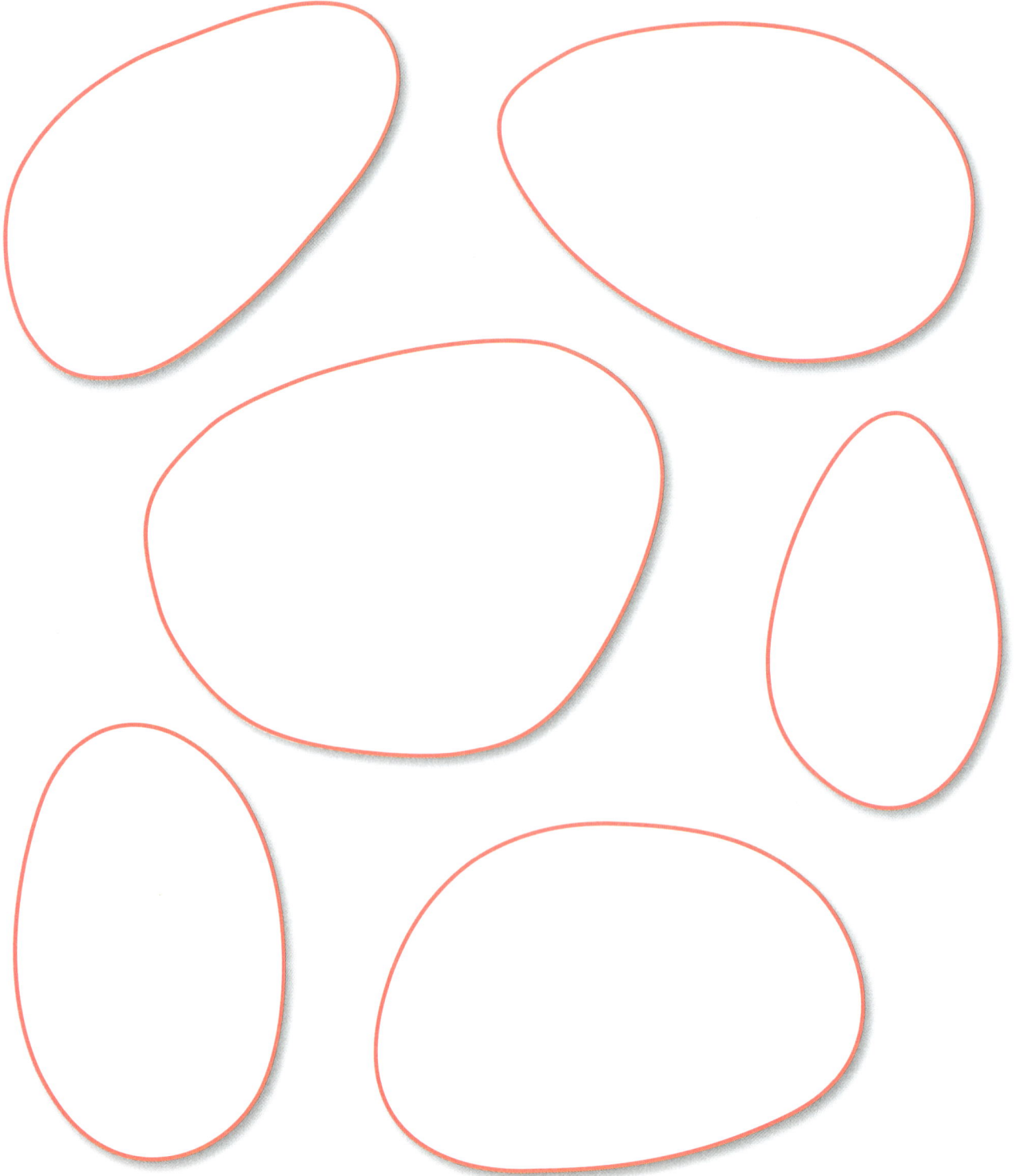

Lesson 2 Other people's feelings

Activity 1.2a What is empathy?

Can you draw some pictures to show what empathy is?

What is empathy?

Lesson 2 Other people's feelings

Activity 1.2b How can I help?

If your friend is upset or in trouble, how could you help them?

Lesson 3 It's OK to feel this way

Activity 1.3 Reflection

Can you name all of the emotions below?

_____

_____

_____

_____

Unit reflection

Can you match the emotion words to the photos? Draw a line from the emotion picture to the matching emotion word.

Excited

Happy

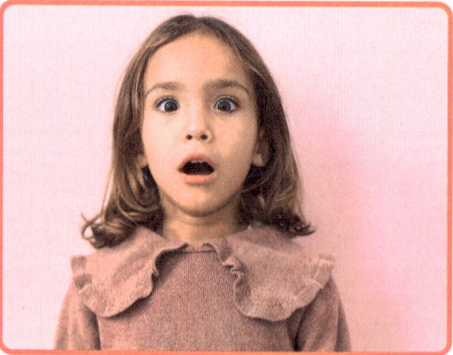

Sad

Shocked

Unit 1.2 Exploring my emotions

What do you know?

- What can you see in the pictures?
- Circle the faces which you think show happiness in yellow and circle the faces which you think show sadness in blue.

In this unit, you will:

- Explore what makes you feel happy and sad.
- Create natural resource faces.
- Tackle some problem-solving challenges.

Lesson 1 What makes me happy or sad?

Activity 2.1a Happy collage

Create your own happy collage. Cut out pictures from magazines, photos or shapes to create your collage.

Lesson 1 What makes me happy or sad?

Activity 2.1b What makes me happy or sad?

In the circles below, write or draw things which make you happy or sad. Remember, if you are ever feeling sad you can talk to your friends, family and your trusted adults.

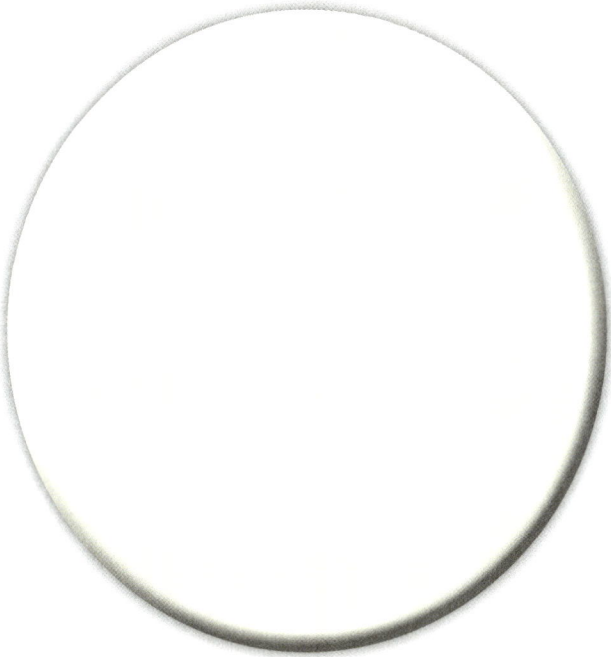

Lesson 2 Don't give up!

Activity 2.2a Animal sudoku

Cut out the animals from Worksheet 1.2.2 to complete your sudoku puzzle. Remember, each animal should only appear once in each column, row and block.

Lesson 2 Don't give up!

Activity 2.2b Problem-solving challenges

Can you complete these challenges in your groups?

Can you complete a jigsaw? ☐

Can you make a bridge using construction blocks? ☐

Can you write as many words as you can think of beginning with the letter 'b'? ☐

Can you design a new game to play? ☐

Can you make up a joke to tell? ☐

Lesson 3 I am unique

Activity 2.3a Things I like

Draw a picture of yourself in the box in the middle and all of the things you like in the circles.

Me!

Lesson 3 I am unique

Activity 2.3b I am so special!

List three things which make you special.

1. _____
   _____
   _____
   _____

2. _____
   _____
   _____
   _____

3. _____
   _____
   _____
   _____

Unit reflection

Colour in the flower using your favourite colours. In the centre of the flower, draw or write some things that you can do to help yourself feel better if you feel sad, want to give up or are feeling some big emotions.

Unit 1.3 Looking after myself

What do you know?
- What can you see in the pictures?
- Can you name each of the foods?
- What foods do you enjoy?
- Are there any foods you don't enjoy as much?

In this unit, you will:
- Explore what foods are good for our bodies.
- Have a disco in your classroom.
- Learn how to brush your teeth correctly.

Lesson 1 Healthy food habits

Activity 3.1a Favourite meal picture

Create a picture of your favourite meal. Ask your friends what their favourite meals are. Do any of them sound delicious? Would you like to try them?

My favourite meal is _____

_____

_____

Lesson 1 Healthy food habits

Activity 3.1b Fruit rockets

Draw the fruit rockets which you created. What fruit did you use? What shape was each piece? What colour was each piece of fruit?

Label each fruit rocket.

Lesson 2 Moving and shaking

Activity 3.2a Exercise

What are your favourite ways to exercise?

Draw pictures in the shapes below.

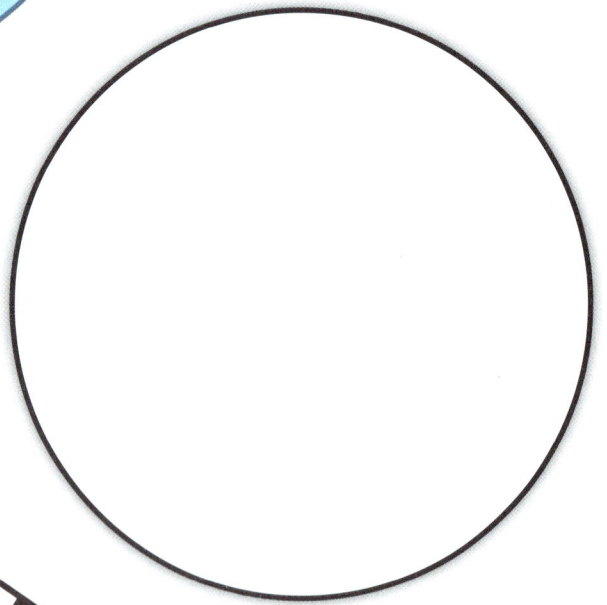

Lesson 2 Moving and shaking

Activity 3.2b I would like to try...

Think about any new sports or movement you would like to try. Draw them below.

Lesson 3 Brush your teeth

Activity 3.3a How should I brush my teeth?

Think about the things you need to do when brushing your teeth properly.
Draw each stage in the boxes below.

Lesson 3 Brush your teeth

Activity 3.3b The teeth-brushing song

Illustrate the words to the teeth-brushing song. What pictures could you draw to show what to do when you brush your teeth?

This is the way we brush our teeth, brush our teeth, brush our teeth.

This is the way we brush our teeth, early in the morning.

We brush our teeth from side to side, side to side, side to side.

We brush our teeth from side to side, so they are nice and clean.

We brush our teeth up and down, up and down, up and down.

We brush our teeth up and down, so they are nice and clean.

This is the way we brush our teeth, brush our teeth, brush our teeth.

This is the way we brush our teeth, before we go to bed.

Unit reflection

In this unit we have been learning about healthy meals, exercise and keeping our teeth clean. Think about the things you have learned and draw or write what you remember below.

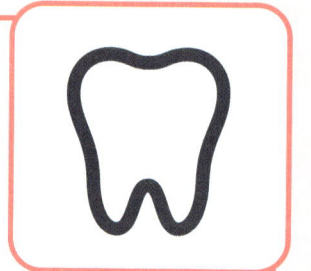

Unit 1.4 People who are special to me

I'm Glad I'm Me

No one looks the way I do,
I have noticed that it's true.
No one walks the way I walk.
No one talks the way I talk.
No one plays the way I play
No one says the things I say.
I am special,
I am Me.
There is no one I would
Rather be
Than Me!

By Jack Prelutsky

What do you know?
- What do you think the poem is about?
- What makes you special?
- Are we all different?

In this unit, you will:
- Draw a comic strip to show a special day in your life.
- Create a friendship bracelet for a friend.
- Explore the ways we can make friends.

Lesson 1 People who love me

Activity 4.1a What we do together

Draw a picture of what activities you like to do with people you love. This might be a picture of somewhere you have been together or an activity you like to share.

Lesson 1 People who love me

Activity 4.1b A special day

Think of a special day that you have spent with someone you love. Draw a comic strip below of what you did.

Lesson 2 We are all the same, we are all different

Activity 4.2a Family celebrations

Draw a picture or make a collage of your family celebrating a special event, day or time in your life.

Lesson 2 We are all the same, we are all different

Activity 4.2b Is it ok to be different?

Look at the sentences below. Do you agree or disagree with them? If you agree, draw a smiley face in the box. If you disagree, draw a sad face in the box.

	Agree or disagree?
If people are different, they can't be friends.	
Being friends with someone who is different from you is interesting as you can learn about someone else's life.	
You should be unkind to people if they are different from you.	
You don't have to agree with your friends all the time.	

Lesson 3 Making friends

Activity 4.3a Friend story

Can you act out the story below with your friends?

What do you think is happening in each of the pictures?

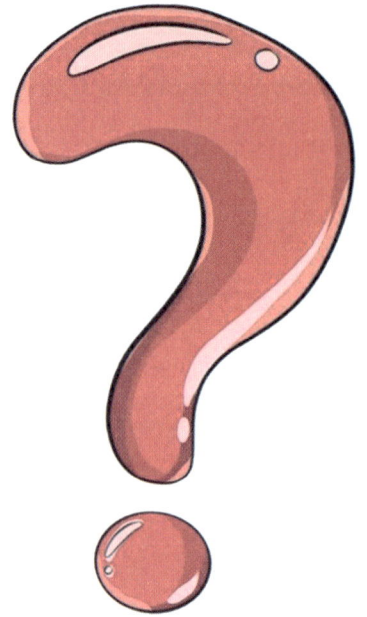

Lesson 3 Making friends

Activity 4.3b Friendship bracelet

Can you design a friendship bracelet for your friend?

What are their favourite colours and patterns?

Draw your design below.

Unit reflection

Think of someone who is your friend.

What do you like to do together?

How do they make you feel? How do you know they are your friend?

Draw or write your answers below.

How my friend
makes me feel

How I like to
spend time with
my friend

How I know they
are my friend

Unit 1.5 Working together

What do you know?

- What is happening in the photo?
- Who is joining in?
- Do you think they know each other?

In this unit, you will:

- Explore ways to make up with friends if you have fallen out.
- Look at a range of communities and share what communities you belong to.
- Agree on some rules for the classroom and design your own school rules.

Lesson 1 Falling out

Activity 5.1 Me apologising

Think of a time when you have apologised. Draw a picture of you apologising.

Which words did you use to apologise?

_____

_____

_____

_____

sorry   forgive   because   apologise
felt   sad   friend

Lesson 2 Our community

Activity 5.2a Our community project

Design a project which can help people. Think about these questions.

Who would you like to help?

How could you help the community?

What might your project look like? Draw a picture of it below.

Lesson 2 Our community

Activity 5.2b What is community?

What do you think about when you hear the word 'community'? What does it mean?

Community

Lesson 3 Rules rule!

Activity 5.3a Silly rules

What silly rules do you think might be fun to try out for a lesson?

Remember, your rule must be silly but not something that could cause someone to get hurt.

Draw a poster to show your silly rule below.

Lesson 3 Rules rule!

Activity 5.3b A super classmate

What makes a super classmate? What do they do that makes them so great?

Draw a picture of your super classmate and all the things they do below.

Lesson 3 Rules rule!

Activity 5.3c My class rule book

Draw the rules of your classroom below. Talk to your talking partner about why each rule is important.

You can write the rule below your drawing if you would like to.

Unit reflection

Create your own school

If you started your own school, what rules would you have?
Think about rules that keep us safe, happy and kind.

My school rules

1.

2.

3.

Unit 1.6 Keeping myself safe

What do you know?

- What can you see in the picture?
- What are all of these things for?
- Who might use these items?

In this unit, you will:

- Learn why rules in the classroom are important.
- Explore ways to keep safe in your home.
- Learn about keeping your personal information safe online.

Lesson 1 Staying safe in school

Activity 6.1 Portrait gallery

Think about the people who keep you safe in school. Draw a picture of adults in school who help to keep you safe.

Lesson 2 Road safety

Activity 6.2a How do you get to school?

Can you create a pictogram to show how children in your class get to school? Use the pictures from Worksheet 1.6.2 to help you.

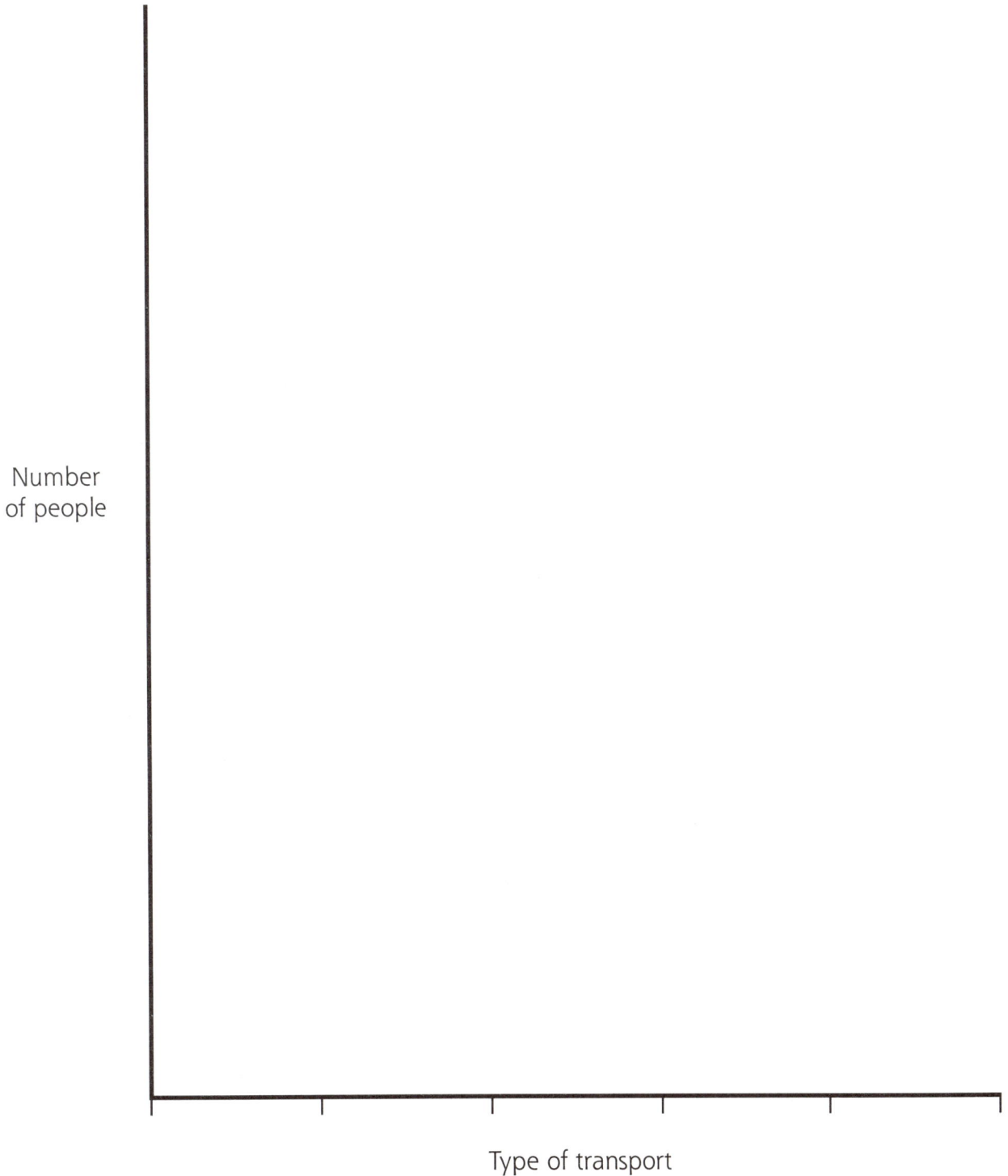

Number of people

Type of transport

Lesson 2 Road safety

Activity 6.2b Different types of transport

Draw a picture of a type of transport. You might like to draw a car, train, aeroplane or tram. Think of the transport you take every week.

Lesson 3 Do I know you?

Activity 6.3a What would you share?

What information would you share with a stranger?

Would you share ...	Yes	No
Your name?		
Your address?		
Your favourite colour?		
The name of your school?		
Your favourite toy?		
Where you have been on holiday?		

Lesson 3 Do I know you?

Activity 6.3b Devices are great

What games or apps do you like to play on your devices? Draw your favourite games below.

9:30

Lesson 3 Do I know you?

Activity 6.3c Top tips

What are your top tips for staying safe online?

Draw your top three tips.

Unit reflection

Discuss with your partner whether the people in the pictures are safe.
Could they do anything different to be safer?

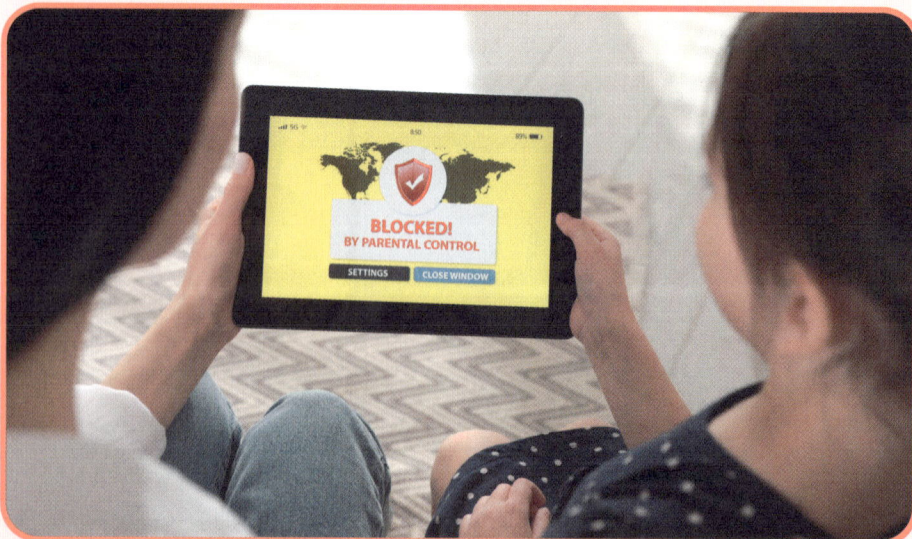

Unit 1.7 I am growing up

What do you know?

- What can you see in the picture?
- What do you think is happening?
- Where do you think you are in the picture?

In this unit, you will:

- Order the life cycle of a human.
- Create 'I can' posters to show all of the things you can do now and would like to do in the future.
- Explore how it feels to move to a different class or year group.

Lesson 1 I am growing

Activity 7.1a Human life cycle

Cut out the pictures from Worksheet 1.7.1. Stick them below in order from youngest to oldest.

Lesson 1 I am growing

Activity 7.1b Time travel scrapbook

Think of the changes that have happened in your life. How did they make you feel?

Draw or write about the changes you have experienced below and how they made you feel. You can start your time travel scrapbook from when you were a baby.

Lesson 2 Being independent

Activity 7.2 I can

Choose some tasks from the lollipop pot or your own ideas and write them in the 'I can' box. How confident do you feel that you can do each task? Draw an emoji in the box to show how confident you feel about each task.

	I can ...

	I can ...

	I can ...

	I can ...

	I can ...

Lesson 3 Moving on up

Activity 7.3a I am proud

I am proud of

because

Lesson 3 Moving on up

Activity 7.3b My new class wish

My wish for my new class is
_____
_____
_____
_____
_____
_____
_____
_____

Lesson 3 Moving on up

Activity 7.3c Tomas's first day

Look at the pictures of Tomas's first day in the purple class. Talk to your talking partner about what is happening in each picture.

How do you think Tomas felt after his first day?

Unit reflection

It's time to reflect on growing up and all the exciting changes that will happen in your life. We know that we can prepare for changes by asking questions, asking for help if we need it and by remembering that it's ok to make mistakes and try again.

Think about the things you are looking forward to as you get older. What are the top three things you are looking forward to as you become more independent?

1. _____
_____
_____
_____
_____
_____

2. _____
_____
_____
_____
_____
_____

3. _____
_____
_____
_____
_____

Unit 1.8 Celebrating difference

What do you know?

- What can you see in the pictures?
- Circle the foods you enjoy and put a cross beside the foods you dislike.

In this unit, you will:

- Find out how chocolate is made and even try some!
- Explore different celebrations and find out what events and occasions your friends celebrate.
- Create friendship bracelets for your friends.

Lesson 1 Where does my food come from?

Activity 8.1a How is chocolate made?

Can you put the pictures in order? Put the number 1 in the box to show which photo is the first in the sequence, then 2 in the second one and so on.

Lesson 1 Where does my food come from?

Activity 8.1b My favourite chocolate

Do you like chocolate?

Draw a picture of your favourite chocolate bar or sweet treat.

Lesson 2 What do you celebrate?

Activity 8.2a What do you like to celebrate?

Draw pictures of the events you like to celebrate.

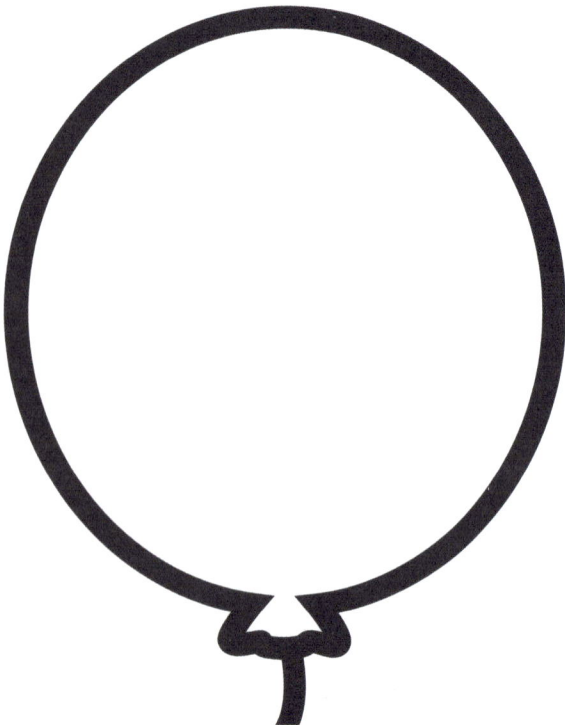

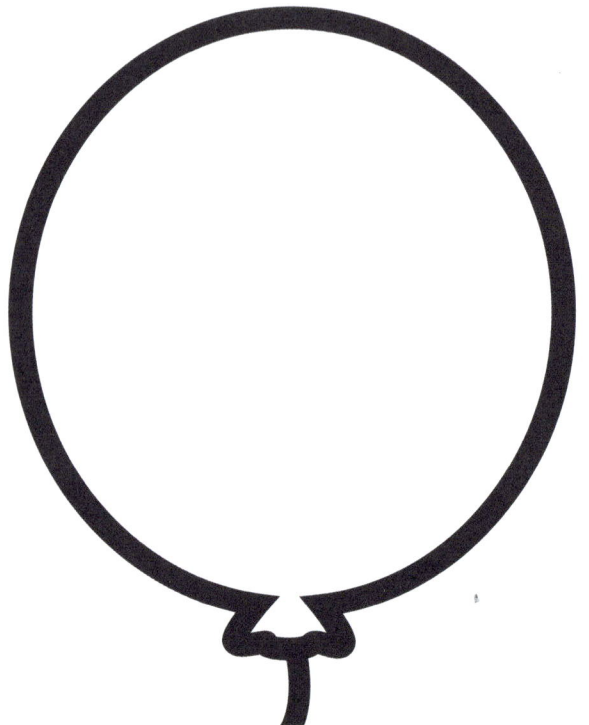

Lesson 2 What do you celebrate?

Activity 8.2b Party time planning

Think about a time when you have celebrated or have been to a party. What decorations or things did you see there?

Imagine you are planning a party. Draw all of the things you might need or the decorations you might design.

Lesson 3 We are all different

Activity 8.3a Similarities and differences

Answer the questions below, then ask a friend the same questions. If any answers are the same, circle them in blue; if any are different, circle them in green. You can write some of your own questions as well.

	My answer	My friend's answer
What is your favourite colour?		
If you could have any superpower, what would it be?		
What is your favourite way to help people?		
What is your favourite thing about school?		
What is your favourite book or story?		

Lesson 3 We are all different

Activity 8.3b What have you learned?

Can you complete the sentence below?

It is great to be different because _____

_____

_____

_____

_____

_____

_____

_____

_____

_____

_____

_____

_____

_____

_____

_____

_____

Unit reflection

Draw a picture of your favourite celebration food.

What makes it special and different from the food you eat every day?

Where do you think the ingredients to make this food comes from?

Acknowledgements

We are grateful to the following for permission to reproduce copyright material:

1.4. The poem "I'm Glad I'm Me" by Jack Prelutsky, as published in I'm glad I'm me – poems about you, Scholastic, 2006, copyright © Jack Prelutsky, 2006. Reproduced by kind permission of the author.
PPT 1.1.3 and SB p.7 *Hello Feelings, Poppy O'Neill, illustrated by Ceej Rowland Reprinted by permission of HarperCollins Publishers Ltd © 2022*
PPT 1.4.1 *Six of Us, Angie Belcher, illustrated by Sylwia Filipczak Reprinted by permission of HarperCollins Publishers Ltd © 2020*
PPT 2.1.3 Slide 2 *I Feel Good, Susan Frame, Reprinted by permission of HarperCollins Publishers Ltd © 2021*
SB 3.2 p. 13 & PPT 3.7.3 Slides 4–6 *Big Feelings, Becky Goddard-Hill, Reprinted by permission of HarperCollins Publishers Ltd © 2023*
PPT 3.7.2 *Martha's Mistake, Poppy O'Neill, Illustrated by Esther Hernando Reprinted by permission of HarperCollins Publishers Ltd © 2022*
SB 3.7 p. 54, WS 3.7.3 & PPT 3.7.3, Slide 3 *Man-Yee and the New School, Mio Debnam, Illustrated by Wendy Tan Shiau Wei Reprinted by permission of HarperCollins Publishers Ltd © 2021*

The publishers wish to thank the following for permission to reproduce images and copyright material. Every effort has been made to trace copyright holders and to obtain their permission for the use of copyright materials. The publishers will gladly receive any information enabling them to rectify any error or omission at the first opportunity.

1.1.1 SB p. 1 Rawpixel.com/Shutterstock, PPT Slide 1 (l&r) Yayayoyo/Shutterstock, SB p. 2 (t) & PPT Slide 2 cougarsan/Shutterstock, p. 2 (m) & PPT Slide 2 ober-art/Shutterstock, SB p. 2 (b) & PPT Slide 2 KVASVECTOR/Shutterstock, SB p. 3 & WS 1.1.1 AyselDesign/Shutterstock, PPT Slide 3 (tl) Prostock-studio/Shutterstock, Slide 3 (tr) iona didishvili/Shutterstock, Slide 3 (b) Roman Samborskyi/Shutterstock, Slide 4 (t) Samuel Borges Photography/Shutterstock, Slide 4 (b) Andrey_Popov/Shutterstock, **1.1.2** WS from My Life – Early Years Foundation Stage Primary PSHE Handbook © HarperCollins Publishers 2022, PPT Slides 1 & 2 Inkley Studio/Shutterstock, Slide 3 Nicoleta Ionescu/Shutterstock, Slide 4 & SB p. 6 BNP Design Studio/Shutterstock, Slide 5 (t) Pongchart B/Shutterstock, Slide 5 (bl) Gorloff-KV/Shutterstock, Slide 5 (br) Phil's Mommy/Shutterstock, **1.1.3** SB p. 8 (1) Monkey Business Images/ Shutterstock, p. 8 (2) pakww/Shutterstock, p. 8 (3) Krakenimages.com/Shutterstock, p. 8 (4) aslysun/Shutterstock, **1.2.1** SB p. 9 Wise ant/Shutterstock, SB p. 10 stevemart/Shutterstock, PPT Slide 1 (t) fazlarabbidesigner350/Shutterstock, Slide 1 (b) Vectorry/Shutterstock, PPT Slide 2 Martial Red/Shutterstock, PPT Slide 3 cosmaa/Shutterstock, **1.2.2** PPT Slides 1 & 2 from My Life – Early Years Foundation Stage Primary PSHE Handbook © HarperCollins Publishers 2022, PPT Slide 3 MidoSemsem/Shutterstock, PPT Slide 4 kulyk/Shutterstock, SB p12 from My Life – Early Years Foundation Stage Primary PSHE Handbook © HarperCollins Publishers 2022, WS 1.2.2 from My Life – Early Years Foundation Stage Primary PSHE Handbook © HarperCollins Publishers 2022, **1.2.3** PPT Slide 1 (tl) Pedal to the Stock/Shutterstock, PPT Slide 1 (tr) Natalia Lisovskaya/Shutterstock, PPT Slide 1 (bl) Nomad_Soul/Shutterstock, PPT Slide 1 (br) OlegRi/Shutterstock, PPT Slide 2 (l) Lopolo/Shutterstock, PPT Slide 2 (r) phipatbig/Shutterstock, PPT Slide 3 Robert Plociennik/Shutterstock, PPT Slide 4 (tr) Buravleva stock/Shutterstock, PPT Slide 4 (tr) bergamont/Shutterstock, PPT Slide 4 (br) Chand.awp/Shutterstock, PPT Slide 4 (bl) Emily Delbetto/Shutterstock, SB p. 15 ma_nud_sen/Shutterstock, SB p. 16 frameeffect/Shutterstock, **1.3.1** SB p. 17 (tr), p. 24 Nungning20/Shutterstock, SB p. 17 (b) Natalia Lisovskaya/Shutterstock, p. 17 (tl) Tatjana Baibakova/Shutterstock, p. 18 Suradech Prapairat/Shutterstock, PPT Slide 1 Foxbrush/Shutterstock, PPT Slide 2 Mary Long/Shutterstock, PPT Slide 2 Nadiyka U/Shutterstock, PPT Slide 2 passionastia/Shutterstock, PPT Slide 2 GoodStudio/Shutterstock, PPT Slide 2 Farah Sadikhova/Shutterstock, PPT Slide 3 Tartila/Shutterstock, PPT Slide 5 Gular Samadova/Shutterstock, SB p. 20 (t) Pavel K/Shutterstock, WS 1.3.1 curiosity/Shutterstock, New Africa/Shutterstock, Nik Merkulov/Shutterstock, monticello/Shutterstock, guy42/Shutterstock, Bukhta Yurii/Shutterstock, PixaHub/Shutterstock, CWIS/Shutterstock, New Africa/Shutterstock, Nasir hameed siddiqui/Shutterstock, andersphoto/Shutterstock, Alter-ego/Shutterstock, Photoongraphy/Shutterstock, studiovin/Shutterstock, WIPHARAT CHAINUPAPHA/Shutterstock, ilolab/Shutterstock, Designs Stock/Shutterstock, Spalnic/Shutterstock, Maks Narodenko/Shutterstock, Charles Brutlag/Shutterstock, baibaz/Shutterstock, Val_R/Shutterstock, Pixel-Shot/Shutterstock, spaxiax/Shutterstock, **1.3.2** PPT Slide 1 from My Life – Early Years Foundation Stage Primary PSHE Handbook © HarperCollins Publishers 2022, PPT Slide 2 Backgroundy/Shutterstock, PPT Slide 2 TinnaPong/Shutterstock, Roman Samborskyi/Shutterstock, Natee K Jindakum/Shutterstock, Stuart Monk/Shutterstock, Rawpixel.com/Shutterstock, Snehal Jeevan Pailkar/Shutterstock, AnnGaysorn/Shutterstock, PPT Slide 3 J.Lapina/Shutterstock, **1.3.3** WS 1.3.3a from My Life – Early Years Foundation Stage Primary PSHE Handbook © HarperCollins Publishers 2022, WS 1.3.3b (tl) BadaL_studio/Shutterstock, WS 1.3.3b (tr) Maksym Drozd/Shutterstock, WS 1.3.3b (b) Sanit Fuangnakhon/Shutterstock, PPT Slide 1 KanKhem/Shutterstock, ianakauri/Shutterstock, Sudowoodo/Shutterstock, PPT Slide 2 Krakenimages.com/Shutterstock, PPT Slide 3 Alena Razumova/Shutterstock, PPT Slide 4 (l) Yesaulov Vadym/Shutterstock, PPT Slide 4 (r) Sketch Master/Shutterstock, SB p. 24 (t) Tatjana Baibakova/Shutterstock, SB p. 24 (m) Nadiyka U/Shutterstock, SB p. 24 (b) Tukunen/Shutterstock, **1.4.1** SB p. 25 mixcolours/Shutterstock, PPT Slide 5 wavebreakmedia/Shutterstock, Evgeny Atamanenko/Shutterstock, photrix/Shutterstock, icon0.com/Shutterstock, oliveromg/Shutterstock, PPT Slide 6 BongkarnGraphic/Shutterstock, AnnGaysorn/Shutterstock, Odua Images/Shutterstock,

SALMONNEGRO-STOCK/Shutterstock, **1.4.2** WS 1.4.2 BlueRingMedia/Shutterstock, Aleksandr_Lysenko/Shutterstock, 1.4.2 WS 1.4.2 from My Life – Early Years Foundation Stage Primary PSHE Handbook © HarperCollins Publishers 2022, PPT Slide 1 wavebreakmedia/Shutterstock, AnnGaysorn/Shutterstock, Valeria Selezneva/Shutterstock, PPT Slide 2 Zolak/Shutterstock, **1.4.3** PPT Slide 1 TY Lim/Shutterstock, Teerawat Anothaistaporn/Shutterstock, MNStudio/Shutterstock, PPT Slide 2, SB p. 30 from My Life – Early Years Foundation Stage Primary PSHE Handbook © HarperCollins Publishers 2022, WS 1.4.3 from My Life – Early Years Foundation Stage Primary PSHE Handbook © HarperCollins Publishers 202, SB p. 32 Tenstudio/Shutterstock, **1.5.1** WS 1.5.1a from My Life – Early Years Foundation Stage Primary PSHE Handbook © HarperCollins Publishers 2022, SB p. 33 Monkey Business Images/ Shutterstock, PPT Slide 2 NassornSnitwong/Shutterstock, PPT Slide 3 BNP Design Studio/Shutterstock, PPT Slide 2 NassornSnitwong/Shutterstock, **1.5.2** PPT Slide 1 justaa/Shutterstock, PPT Slide 2 Olga1818/Shutterstock, FGC/Shutterstock, Sensvector/Shutterstock, PPT Slide 3 MUHAMMAD ASNAWI 15/Shutterstock, Chanintorn.v/Shutterstock, Anna Nass/Shutterstock, Kaarthikeyan.SM/Shutterstock, PPT Slide 4 Simply Amazing/Shutterstock, elenabsl/Shutterstock, YUCALORA/Shutterstock, Midorie/Shutterstock, **1.5.3** WS 1.5.3 from My Life – Early Years Foundation Stage Primary PSHE Handbook © HarperCollins Publishers 2022, PPT Slide 1 BNP Design Studio/Shutterstock, PPT Slide 2 omravestudio/Shutterstock, PPT Slide 3 Macrovector/Shutterstock, PPT Slide 4 t sr-art studio/Shutterstock, Slide 4 bl Nicoleta Ionescu/Shutterstock, Slide 4 bm azmeyart/Shutterstock, Slide 4 br from My Life – Early Years Foundation Stage Primary PSHE Handbook © HarperCollins Publishers 2022, PPT Slide 5 Andrei Shumskiy/Shutterstock, SB p. 38 Olga1818/Shutterstock, SB p. 39 BNP Design Studio/Shutterstock, SB p. 39 Andrey_Kuzmin/Shutterstock, SB p. 40 lineartestpilot/Shutterstock, **1.6.1** SB p. 41 Bonezboyz/Shutterstock, SB p. 42 stevemart/Shutterstock, PPT Slide 1 Ground Picture/Shutterstock, Gary L Hider/Shutterstock, Twinsterphoto/Shutterstock, Nok Lek Travel Lifestyle/Shutterstock, PPT Slide 2 & Slide 3 Granate Art/Shutterstock, PPT Slide 4 & Slide 5 BNP Design Studio/Shutterstock, **1.6.2** PPT Slide 1 Sri Rahmi Purnamasari/Shutterstock, Art Konovalov/Shutterstock, James Jiao/Shutterstock, ANURAK PONGPATIMET/Shutterstock, Juntee/Shutterstock, PPT Slide 2 from My Life – Early Years Foundation Stage Primary PSHE Handbook © HarperCollins Publishers 2022, PPT Slide 3 Joko SL/Shutterstock, Philip Lange/Shutterstock, Ann in the uk/Shutterstock, Ruud Suhendar/Shutterstock, WS 1.6.2 matsabe/Shutterstock, AAVAA/Shutterstock, M-vector/Shutterstock, Janis Abolins/Shutterstock, kokank13/Shutterstock, BalMak/Shutterstock, Dshnrgc/Shutterstock, **1.6.3** SB p. 46 Carkhe/Shutterstock, SB p. 47 Lemberg Vector studio/Shutterstock, SB p. 48 pavla/Shutterstock, BNP Design Studio/Shutterstock, William Perugini/Shutterstock, New Africa/Shutterstock, PPT Slide 1 Mustafa Kemal Bolukbasi/Shutterstock, Sasha Ka/Shutterstock, BGStock72/Shutterstock, canbedone/Shutterstock, PPT Slide 2 Sergey Novikov/Shutterstock, PPT Slide 3 fizkes/Shutterstock, **1.7.1** SB p. 49 & PPT 1.7.1 Slide 1 GoodStudio/Shutterstock, WS 1.7.1 GoodStudio/Shutterstock, SB p. 51 Lemonade Serenade/ Shutterstock, PPT Slide 2 GoodStudio/Shutterstock, PPT Slide 3 Stratos Giannikos/Shutterstock, **1.7.2** PPT Slide 1 Colorfuel Studio/Shutterstock, PPT Slide 2 didesign021/Shutterstock, Odua Images/Shutterstock, Aleksei Potov/Shutterstock, PPT Slide 3 GraphicsRF.com/Shutterstock, **1.7.3** SB p. 56 Prostock-studio/Shutterstock, SB p. 55 & PPT slides 1 & 3 from My Life – Early Years Foundation Stage Primary PSHE Handbook © HarperCollins Publishers 2022, PPT Slide 2 Prostock-studio/Shutterstock, PPT Slide 4 Alano Design/Shutterstock, **1.8.1** SB p. 57 & PPT Slide 1 Oksana Mizina/Shutterstock, SB p. 57 beats1/Shutterstock, Losangela/Shutterstock, Tatjana Baibakova/Shutterstock, PPT Slide 1 Elena Veselova/Shutterstock, Timolina/Shutterstock, ba55ey/Shutterstock, addiduu/Shutterstock, PPT Slide 2 & SB p. 58 BestForBest/Shutterstock, PPT Slide 2 & SB p. 58 Aedka Studio/Shutterstock, PPT Slide 2 & SB p. 58 noBorders – Brayden Howie/Shutterstock, PPT Slide 2 & SB p. 58 Chad Zuber/Shutterstock, PPT Slide 2 & SB p. 58 Maria_Ermolenko/Shutterstock, WS 1.8.1 BestForBest/Shutterstock, Aedka Studio/Shutterstock, noBorders – Brayden Howie/Shutterstock, Chad Zuber/Shutterstock, Maria_Ermolenko/Shutterstock, SB p. 59 Its design/Shutterstock, PPT Slide 3 johavel/Shutterstock, pockygallery/Shutterstock, Onica Alexandru Sergiu/Shutterstock, Awesome_art_Creation/Shutterstock, Janos Levente/Shutterstock, YummyBuum/Shutterstock, **1.8.2** SB p. 60 galaira/Shutterstock, SB p. 61 Wise ant/Shutterstock, PPT Slide 1 Thomas M Perkins/Shutterstock, DGLimages/Shutterstock, Drazen Zigic/Shutterstock, SeventyFour/Shutterstock, Gatot Adri/Shutterstock, T.TATSU/Shutterstock, HM Shahidul Islam/Shutterstock, PPT Slide 3 SPSTL/Shutterstock, **1.8.3** SB p. 63 BNP Design Studio/Shutterstock, SB p. 64 Ruth Black/Shutterstock, Dina Saeed/Shutterstock, WS 1.8.3a stockvit/ Shutterstock, Pro Symbols/ Shutterstock, Viktorija Reuta/ Shutterstock, Warmworld/ Adobe stock, Tassia_K/ Shutterstock, EPS/ Shutterstock. **2.1.1** SB p. 1 Katerina Davidenko/Shutterstock, Wat cartoon/Shutterstock, KanKhem/Shutterstock, PPT Slide 1 roshenshami/Shutterstock, By PeopleImages.com – Yuri A/Shutterstock, PPT Slide 3 CGN089/Shutterstock, Nicoleta Ionescu/Shutterstock, PPT Slide 4 Bibadash/Shutterstock, **2.1.2** SB p. 3, PPT slides 1-3 & 5-6 from My Life – Key Stage 1 Primary PSHE Handbook © HarperCollins Publishers 2022, PPT Slide 4 SeventyFour/Shutterstock, PPT Slide 7 yusufdemirci/Shutterstock, **2.1.3** SB p. 6 Hakase_420/Shutterstock, SB p. 6 PeopleImages.com – Yuri A/Shutterstock, WS 2.1.3 Hakase_420/Shutterstock, PeopleImages.com – Yuri A/Shutterstock, PPT Slide 1 icon Stocker/Shutterstock, PPT Slide 2 MorganStudio/Shutterstock, PPT Slide 3 shopplaywood/Shutterstock, PPT Slide 4 GoodStudio/Shutterstock, **2.2.1** SB p. 9 yusufdemirci/Shutterstock, Shysheep/Shutterstock, PPT Slide 1 Queenmoonlite Studio/Shutterstock, PPT Slide 2 Anna Nahabed/Shutterstock, PPT Slide 3 Vitalii Petrenko/Shutterstock, PPT Slide 5 svtdesign/Shutterstock, **2.2.2** WS 2.2.2 ANNA ZASIMOVA/Shutterstock, PPT Slide 1 Natalie Osipova/Shutterstock, PPT Slide 2 Shysheep (duplicate)/Shutterstock, PPT Slide 3 HappyPictures/Shutterstock, Orawan Wongka/Shutterstock, Bibadash/Shutterstock, **2.2.3** PPT Slide 1 Bibadash/Shutterstock, PPT Slide 2 Muhammad Desta Laksana/Shutterstock, PPT Slide 3 primiaou/Shutterstock, PPT Slide 4 Mus Illustrations/Shutterstock, **2.3.1** SB p. 17 Wanwisspaul/Shutterstock, PPT Slide 1 Ami Parikh/Shutterstock, 220 Selfmade studio/Shutterstock, Slides 1 & 3 s_oleg/Shutterstock, PPT Slide 2 eamesBot/Shutterstock, **2.3.2** SB p. 20 & PPT Slide 2 yut548/Shutterstock, PPT Slide 1 Spotmatik Ltd/Shutterstock, Remen Explore/Shutterstock, PPT Slide 3 from My Life – Key Stage 1 Primary PSHE Handbook © HarperCollins Publishers 2022, PPT Slide 4 from My

Life – Key Stage 1 Primary PSHE Handbook © HarperCollins Publishers 2022, PPT Slide 5 HowLettery/Shutterstock, **2.3.3** PPT Slide 1 In-Finity/Shutterstock, PPT Slide 2 LightField Studios/Shutterstock, Serhiy Kobyakov/Shutterstock, Pixel-Shot/Shutterstock, kosmofish/Shutterstock, Slide 3 yusufdemirci/Shutterstock, Slide 4 from My Life – Early Years Foundation Stage Primary PSHE Handbook © HarperCollins Publishers 2022, WS 2.3.3 from My Life – Early Years Foundation Stage Primary PSHE Handbook © HarperCollins Publishers 2022, SB p. 22 BNP Design Studio/Shutterstock, SB p. 24 girafchik/Shutterstock, **2.4 1** PPT Slide 1 LeManna/Shutterstock, PPT Slide 2 myboys.me/Shutterstock, PPT Slide 3 New Africa/Shutterstock, PPT Slide 4 Antonov Maxim/Shutterstock, Iconic Bestiary/Shutterstock, **2.4.2** PPT Slide 1 YanzStudio/Shutterstock, PPT Slide 2 Rawpixel.com/Shutterstock, PPT Slide 3 Anuta23/Shutterstock, PPT Slide 4 Teerawat Anothaistaporn/Shutterstock, SB p. 25 mixcolours/ Shutterstock, SB p. 29 TinnaPong/Shutterstock, **2.4 3** PPT Slide 1 locrifa/Shutterstock, PPT Slide 2 Scc.comics/ Shutterstock, PPT Slide 3 missisliris/Shutterstock, PPT Slide 4 Zdravinjo/Shutterstock, SewCreamStudio/ Shutterstock, SB p. 30 Colorfuel Studio/Shutterstock, SB p. 32 tanyabosyk/Shutterstock, **2.5 1** SB p. 33 Tartila/ Shutterstock, PPT Slide 1 Elena_Dig/Shutterstock, Slide 2 Roman Samborskyi/Shutterstock, didesign021/Shutterstock, Sergiy Bykhunenko/Shutterstock, hareluya/Shutterstock, PPT Slide 3 wee dezign/Shutterstock, PPT Slide 4 Novikov Alex/Shutterstock, Prostock-studio/ Shutterstock, **2.5.2** PPT Slide 1 New Africa/Shutterstock, PPT Slide 5 StockPhotosLV/Shutterstock, Orawan Wongka/Shutterstock, SB p. 36 WindAwake/ Shutterstock, **2.5 3** PPT Slide 1 mentalmind/Shutterstock, PPT Slide 2 Yana Lesiuk/Shutterstock, PPT Slide 4 cosmaa/Shutterstock, **2.6 1** SB p. 41 GoodStudio/Shutterstock, SB p. 42 stevemart/ Shutterstock, PPT Slide 1 Davidenco / Shutterstock, PPT Slides 3, 4 & 5 AVA Bitter/Shutterstock, PPT Slide 6 MoonRock/Shutterstock, **2.6 2** PPT Slide 1 emka angelina/Shutterstock, PPT slides 4-7 from My Life – Lower Key Stage 2 Primary PSHE Handbook © HarperCollins Publishers 2020, SB p. 45 WikaGraphic/Shutterstock, WS 2.6.2 WikaGraphic/Shutterstock, SB p. 47 3d Jesus/Shutterstock, SB p. 47 3d Jesus/Shutterstock, **2.6.3** PPT Slide 1 Alfmaler/Shutterstock, PPT Slide 1 Mangostar/Shutterstock, Sophon Nawit/Shutterstock, Joe MoJo/Shutterstock, PPT Slide 2 Dmitry Naumov/Shutterstock, Dariusz Jarzabek/Shutterstock, Lifestyle Travel/Shutterstock Photo/Shutterstock, OlegD/Shutterstock, Yevhenii Chulovskyi/Shutterstock, Valentina Razumova/Shutterstock, PPT Slide 3 Zahrotul Fuadah/Shutterstock, PPT Slide 4 Joe MoJo/Shutterstock, PPT Slide 5 garagestock/Shutterstock, SB p. 48 Prostock-studio/Shutterstock, SB p. 48 sutadimages/Shutterstock, SB p. 48 Evgeny Atamanenko/Shutterstock, SB p. 48 Zhuravlev Andrey/Shutterstock, **2.7 1** SB p. 49 ayelet-keshet/Shutterstock, SB p. 51 Art Alex/Shutterstock, PPT Slide 1 tovovan/Shutterstock, Mary Long/Shutterstock, aslysun/Shutterstock, yusufdemirci/Shutterstock, PPT Slide 2 Skoles/Shutterstock, linear_design/Shutterstock, PPT Slide 3 WESTOCK PRODUCTIONS/Shutterstock, **2.7.2** SB p. 53 AlexHliv/Shutterstock, PPT Slide 1 Marish/Shutterstock, PPT Slide 2 Party people studio/Shutterstock, abrikaSimf/Shutterstock, yurakrasil/Shutterstock, PPT Slide 3 MalikNalik/Shutterstock, Manop Boonpeng/Shutterstock, adriaticfoto/Shutterstock, PPT Slide 4 Lano Lan/Shutterstock, Paul Brewer/Shutterstock, Tyler Olson/Shutterstock, PPT Slide 5 wavebreakmedia/Shutterstock, Krakenimages.com/Shutterstock, Nejron Photo/Shutterstock, **2.7 3** PPT Slide 1 & SB p. 54 Isaac Cedercrantz/Shutterstock, PPT Slide 2 Gatot Adri/Shutterstock, yournameonstones/Shutterstock, PPT Slide 3 Brumarina/Shutterstock, PPT Slide 4 Aquir/Shutterstock, **2.8 1** SB p. 57 Yakov Oskanov/Shutterstock, Dmitry Rukhlenko/Shutterstock, Yakov Oskanov/Shutterstock, BGSmith/ Shutterstock, SB p. 58 NatSarunyoo536/Shutterstock, PPT Slide 1 Voyagerix/Shutterstock, Kevin Eaves/Shutterstock, Winston Springwater/Shutterstock, photobobs/Shutterstock, PPT Slide 2 Dzmitrock/Shutterstock, Anton Gvozdikov/Shutterstock, Summit Art Creations/ Shutterstock, xavitorrents/Shutterstock, PPT Slide 3 Andrii_Lomovskii/Shutterstock, Rich Carey/Shutterstock, PPT Slide 4 Ashley-Belle Burns/Shutterstock, PPT Slide 5 Larina Marina/Shutterstock, Petro Perutskyi/Shutterstock, PPT Slide 6 NeoBuu/Shutterstock, Dancake/Shutterstock, 7th Son Studio/Shutterstock, MaraZe/Shutterstock, Tribalium/Shutterstock, Vectorbum/Shutterstock, **2.8.2** PPT Slide 1 BOOCYS/Shutterstock, PPT Slide 2 BOOCYS/Shutterstock, PPT Slide 2 & SB p. 59 spiral media/Shutterstock, WS 2.8.2 spiral media/Shutterstock, SB p. 60 Guilhem Menard/Shutterstock, PPT Slides 2–4 mimagephotography/Shutterstock, PPT Slides 2–4 Krakenimages.com/Shutterstock, PPT Slide 5 AtlasStudio/Shutterstock, rzarek/Shutterstock, Maria_Usp/Shutterstock, karen roach/Shutterstock, Anton Starikov/Shutterstock, **2.8 3** SB p. 63 Icons Home/Shutterstock, PPT Slides 1 & 2 Everett Collection/Shutterstock, Everett Collection/Shutterstock, PPT Slides 1 & 2 catwalker/Shutterstock, neftali/Shutterstock, Janusz Pienkowski/Shutterstock, PPT Slide 3 ANDREI ASKIRKA/Shutterstock, PPT Slide 4 Alex Gorka/Shutterstock, PedroNevesDesign/Shutterstock, MisterStock/Shutterstock **3.1.1** SB p. 1 Iconic Bestiary/Shutterstock, Julia Soul Art/Shutterstock, SB p. 4 & PPT Slide 3 logistock/Shutterstock, PPT Slide 2 ClassicVector/Shutterstock, **3.1.2** WS 3.1.2 Lasha Kilasonia/ Shutterstock, PPT Slide 1 Nailia Schwarz/Shutterstock, PPT Slide 2 Macrovector/Shutterstock, PPT Slide 3 Rawpixel.com/Shutterstock, PPT Slide 4 iris828/Shutterstock, **3.1.3** PPT Slide 1 cute2u/Shutterstock, BRO.vector/Shutterstock, PPT Slide 3 bilha golan/Shutterstock, **3.2.1** SB p. 9 A Sharma/Shutterstock, SB p. 10 Ken Vail, PPT Slide 2 Yaelaaboi/Shutterstock, FoxyImage/Shutterstock, PPT Slide 3 iris828/Shutterstock, Lunarts Studio/Shutterstock, PPT Slide 4 Prostock-studio/Shutterstock, **3.2.2** PPT slide 1 Vectors bySkop/Shutterstock, PPT Slide 2 vectorlab2D/Shutterstock, PPT Slide 3 & SB p. 13 New Africa/Shutterstock, **3.2.3** PPT Slide 1 Shysheep/Shutterstock, PPT Slide 2 Yana Alisovna/Shutterstock, PPT Slide 3 3DBear/Shutterstock, abstract/Shutterstock, mirajeee/Shutterstock, WS 3.2.3a Christina Designs/Shutterstock, WS 3.2.3b Christina Designs/Shutterstock, **3.3.1** SB p. 17 A3pfamily/ Shutterstock, SB p. 18 Realstockvector/Shutterstock, PPT Slide 1 BNP Design Studio/Shutterstock, MegaShabanov/Shutterstock, Aigul Garaeva/Shutterstock, BNP Design Studio/Shutterstock, PPT Slide 2 idham djuanda/Shutterstock, Samuel Borges Photography/Shutterstock, Streamlight Studios/Shutterstock, Slide 2 Pvince73/Shutterstock, **3.3.2** PPT Slide 1 Buravleva stock/Shutterstock, PPT Slide 2 serazetdinov/Shutterstock, Alfmaler/Shutterstock, Daria Shane/Shutterstock, Slide 3 DeymosHR/Shutterstock, PPT Slide 4 e14eak90/Shutterstock, MarySan/Shutterstock, ProStockStudio/Shutterstock, Natykach Nataliia/Shutterstock, OrangeVector/Shutterstock, SB p. 21 reddish/Shutterstock, **3.3.3** SB p. 23 pedrorsfernandes/Shutterstock, PPT Slide 1 GraphicsRF.com/Shutterstock, GoodStudio/

Acknowledgements

Shutterstock, PPT Slide 2 silimoma/Shutterstock, PPT Slide 3 Alexandra B Dolgova/Shutterstock, Studio_G/Shutterstock, Irina Dias/Shutterstock, TINA NIZOVA/Shutterstock, **3.4.1** SB p. 25 Devotion/Shutterstock, SB p. 28 Emilia Dragomir/Shutterstock, WS 3.4.1 Emilia Dragomir/Shutterstock, PPT Slide 1 BNP Design Studio/Shutterstock, PPT Slide 2 GoodStudio/Shutterstock, PPT Slide 3 HowLettery/Shutterstock, PPT Slide 4 GoodStudio/Shutterstock, PPT Slide 5 Marish/Shutterstock, PPT Slide 6 Marben/Shutterstock, GQ/Shutterstock, Dragana Gordic/Shutterstock, **3.4.2** PPT Slide 1 tynyuk/Shutterstock, PPT Slide 2 Monkey Business Images/Shutterstock, wavebreakmedia/Shutterstock, CREATISTA/Shutterstock, legenda/Shutterstock, PPT Slide 3 ann131313.s/Shutterstock, PPT slide 4 Image Source Collection/Shutterstock, PPT Slide 5 Kakigori Studio/Shutterstock, **3.4.3** PPT Slide 1 urbanbuzz/Shutterstock, PPT Slide 4 ayelet-keshet/Shutterstock, **3.5.1** SB p. 33 pathdoc/Shutterstock, SB p. 33 Anna Kraynova/Shutterstock, Ground Picture/Shutterstock, SB p. 34 ZeinousGDS/Shutterstock, PPT Slide 1 oneinchpunch/Shutterstock, Monkey Business Images/Shutterstock, PPT Slide 2 Pavel Kukol/Shutterstock, PPT Slide 3 Drazen Zigic/Shutterstock, PPT Slide 4 AlessandroBiascioli/Shutterstock, imtmphoto/Shutterstock, **3.5.2** SB p. 36 Vitalii Vodolazskyi/Shutterstock, PPT Slide 1 phoelixDE/Shutterstock, PPT Slide 2 MIA Studio/Shutterstock, adriaticfoto/Shutterstock, Sharomka/Shutterstock, AJP/Shutterstock, PPT Slide 4 ClassicVector/Shutterstock, SB p. 37 & PPT Slide 5 iQoncept/Shutterstock, **3.5.3** PPT Slide 1 Sensvector/Shutterstock, PPT Slide 2 HilaryDesign/Shutterstock, PPT Slide 3 mentalmind/Shutterstock, PPT Slide 4 bsd studio/Shutterstock, Slide 5 Colorfuel Studio/Shutterstock, SB p. 40 Prostock-studio/Shutterstock, **3.6.1** SB p. 41 Jacob_09/Shutterstock, paulista/Shutterstock, Efimova Anna/Shutterstock, SB p. 42 & WS 3.6.1 Dmitry Naumov/Shutterstock, SB p. 42 & PPT Slide 4 & WS 3.6.1 The_Molostock/Shutterstock, SB p. 42 & WS 3.6.1 Maidannikov/Shutterstock, SB p. 42 & WS 3.6.1 siridhata/Shutterstock, SB p. 42 & WS 3.6.1 Vitaly Titov/Shutterstock, SB p. 42 & WS 3.6.1 GinaVector/Shutterstock, SB p. 42 & PPT Slide 4 & WS 3.6.1 Anastasia Samorodova/Shutterstock, PPT Slide 2 solar22/Shutterstock, PPT Slide 3 oligganko/Shutterstock, PPT Slide 4 Andrienko Anastasiya/Shutterstock, Adragan/Shutterstock, **3.6.2** SB p. 43, PPT slides 3-4 from My Life – Key Stage 1 Primary PSHE Handbook © HarperCollins Publishers 2022, SB p. 44 o_m/Shutterstock, WS 3.6.2 o_m/Shutterstock, PPT slide 2 Art Kovalenco/Shutterstock, **3.6.3** SB p. 46 & PPT Slide 1 Bojani/Shutterstock, PPT Slide 2 Nikolaeva/Shutterstock, PPT Slide 3 chinahbzyg/Shutterstock, ivnard/Shutterstock, SN040288/Shutterstock, Carsten Schlipf/Shutterstock, PPT Slide 4 YuliaShvetsova/Shutterstock, Nicoleta Ionescu/Shutterstock, PPT Slide 5 Alexey V Smirnov/Shutterstock, SB p. 48 Krisztian/Shutterstock, **3.7.1** SB p. 49 GoodStudio/Shutterstock, SB p. 50 phipatbig/Shutterstock, WS 3.7.1 phipatbig/Shutterstock, PPT Slide 2 Tiko Aramyan/Shutterstock, **3.7.2** PPT Slide 1 ankomando/Shutterstock, PPT Slide 3 Oleksandr Rybitskiy/Shutterstock, PPT Slide 4 Dusica VK/Shutterstock, SB p. 53 v_kulieva/Shutterstock, **3.7.3** PPT Slide 1 fizkes/Shutterstock, PPT Slide 4 Mangkorn Danggura/Shutterstock, PPT Slide 5 Natewimon Nantiwat/Shutterstock, PPT Slide 6 iofoto/Shutterstock, PPT Slide 7 EleniVasiliou/Shutterstock, SB p. 55 Vasilyeva Elada/Shutterstock, SB p. 56 OlgaKlyushina/Shutterstock, **3.8.1** SB p. 57 max dallocco/Shutterstock, PPT Slide 2 ISSARET YATSOMBOON/Shutterstock, PPT Slides 3 & 4 Robert Kneschke/Shutterstock, **3.8.2** PPT Slide 1 MillaF/Shutterstock, PPT Slide 2 Maike Hildebrandt/Shutterstock, SB p. 59 Mallinka1/Shutterstock, WS 3.8.2 Mallinka1/Shutterstock, PPT Slide 3 & SB p. 60 Hari_Aprianto/Shutterstock, SB p. 61 New Africa/Shutterstock, Roman Zaiets/Shutterstock, TaraPatta/Shutterstock, **3.8.3** PPT Slide 3 sarayut_sy/Shutterstock, PPT Slide 4 viki2win/Shutterstock, PPT Slide 5 Katho Menden/Shutterstock, PPT Slide 5 MERCURY studio/Shutterstock.